Let's Explore
Sharks

Michael Patrick O'Neill
Batfish Books

*To Pietro E. Berardi,
Best Wishes!
MPO'Neill*

O'Neill, Michael Patrick
Let's Explore Sharks / Michael Patrick O'Neill
ISBN 978-0-9728653-1-9
LCCN 2005901567

Cover, Graphics & Illustrations: George Milek
Printed in China

Batfish Books
PO Box 32909
Palm Beach Gardens, FL 33420-2909
www.batfishbooks.com
Photographer's Website:
www.mpostock.com

10 9 8 7 6 5 4 3 2

The stinky bait goes overboard...

AND beFore LONg, a Large FiN appears

and circles the boat.

The crew is waiting
for you to get
in the cage.

Are you ready?

WeLL, are you?

To Explore the Wonderful World of Sharks!

Shaped over millions of years, sharks are among the planet's alpha predators. These great fish are all power, grace and mystery.

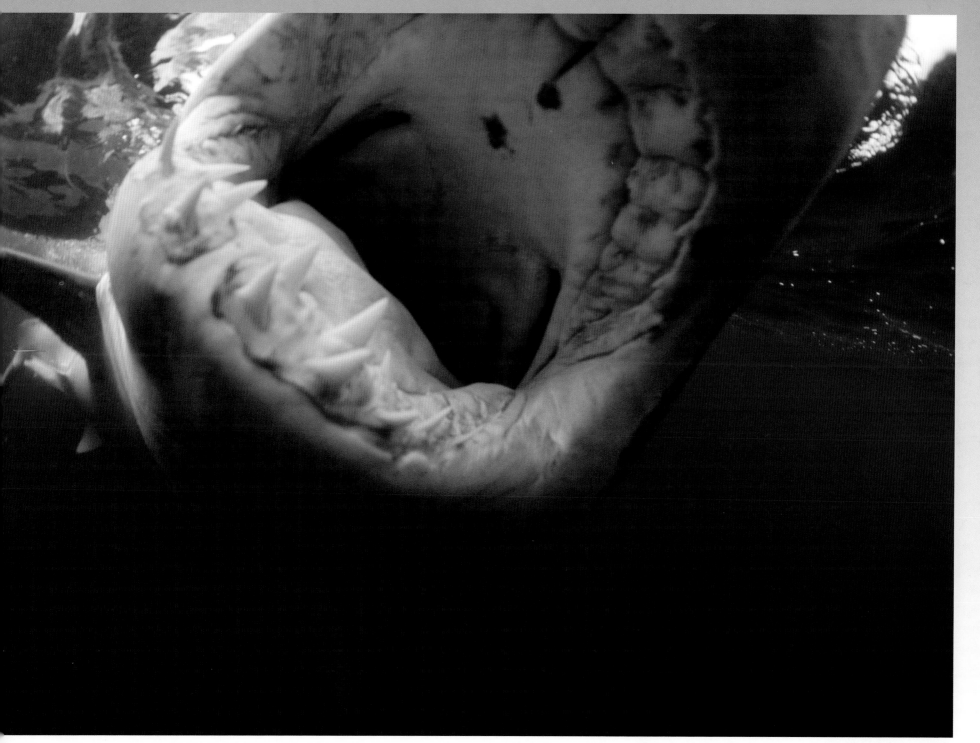

Great white shark

Great White Wonder

Great Whites get their name from their big white bellies. Among the largest fish in the sea, they roam both cool and warm waters worldwide.

They reach 21 ft. and can weigh more than 5,000 lbs. With that massive bulk and sharp teeth two-inches long, they have few enemies: killer whales, other great whites and man.

Hunted for decades, this species is endangered and may become extinct in certain locations. Thankfully, though, some countries with sizeable white shark populations, the U.S., Australia and South Africa, now protect it.

Better late than never!

White sharks are warm-blooded, which gives them the explosive energy they need when hunting.

Fast Food

Seals are among the great whites' favorite meals. These little fur balls are high-energy snacks that help the sharks survive in cold waters.

South African fur seal

Keep in mind great whites work really hard to catch seals. These mammals are super-smart and a tough match for our toothy friends. In fact, most seals never get caught.

It's important to realize that without "Whitey," the marine environment would be unbalanced and unhealthy, with too many seals.

To make it from their rocky islands to the feeding grounds in the open ocean and back, the seals must pass through a treacherous area known as the "killing zone."

This is where danger lurks. Seals must always be on the lookout and at the first sign of danger, scramble to safety. Those not paying attention may not have the chance to make the same mistake twice.

The Scavenger

The Tiger Shark roams near and far in search of a meal — any meal.

Closing in at 20 ft. and 2,000 lbs., the tiger is a tropical hunter identified by its spots and stripes.

This dangerous shark is called the "swimming garbage can" because it eats practically everything in its path, from natural prey to litter.

It also loves to see the world. One tagged in Hawaii was later caught in the Sea of Cortez in Mexico, a distance of 3,000 miles. The habits of the traveling tiger show how extraordinary these fish are and how our marine environment is all connected.

A large female tiger shark cruises the cool waters off South Africa. By the way, in the shark world, the girls are usually bigger and stronger than the boys.

THE GENTLE GIANT

THE WHALE SHARK, THE HEAVYWEIGHT OF THE FAMILY, IS FULL OF SURPRISES.

At 40 ft. and a mind-boggling 26,000 lbs., it's the largest fish on the planet.

In one of nature's many strange twists, this friendly monster eats only small organisms, like plankton and sardines. Tiny teeth, lined up in over 300 rows, and filters near its gills help separate the food from the seawater.

More interesting tidbits about this leviathan: It produces the largest litter among sharks and beats the tiger by a mile – actually many more – when it comes to wandering vast stretches of ocean. A few tagged specimens journeyed 14,000 miles during a 3-year period.

Even a 20 ft. whale shark dwarfs a person.

A Shadow in the Sea

The Great Hammerhead is like a living sculpture, one of the natural world's masterpieces.

With a little imagination, it's easy to think of the great hammerhead as a stealth fighter patrolling the coral reef.

Reaching 20 ft. and weighing up to 1,000 lbs., it's the largest in the family of hammerhead sharks, which includes nine species.

The strange, winged head seems puzzling, but it's no design flaw. The great hammerhead uses it to attack stingrays, and it may also help the shark turn faster and improve its sense of smell.

The Stealth Fighter and the great Hammerhead Share Similar MiSSions.

Avoiding detection by enemies or prey is the name of the game. While the fighter jet relies on 21st century technology, the shark's prehistoric low tech is also extremely sophisticated.

Its tiny sensors allow it to smell – even feel – its quarry from great distances and to close in unseen.

The hammerhead is nature's ultimate all-weather interceptor, a deadly hunter in clear or cloudy water, day or night.

AMbaSSadOrs oF the De

Nurse and Sandbar Sharks help aquariums educate the public on the importance of having very Sharky oceans.

Sandbar sharks have unfortunately been fished out in many areas. They're relatively small, muscular animals around 6 ft. and 200 lbs., and live in both tropical and temperate regions. Although it looks like your "typical shark," the sandbar can be identified by the big, wide fin on its back.

These two species are fighting in the frontlines for the conservation of all sharks. Interestingly enough, part of this battle isn't taking place in the high seas, but in public aquariums worldwide.

It's where thousands come to see these predators and learn about their uncertain future due to overfishing.

With these two hardy soldiers, aquariums hope to turn the tide in favor of sharks and change public opinion.

Nurse sharks are bottom-dwelling, warm-water creatures that look like huge cat-fish with their whiskers right next to the powerful jaws, used to crush lobster and conch. Reaching 11 ft. and about 300 lbs., they like to hide inside coral caves during the day. Considered harmless, on occasion they bite divers who pull on their tails.

NOW, WOULDN'T YOU, TOO?

MISCHIEF MAKERS

Caribbean Reef Sharks are the troublemakers of the coral Kingdom.

Fishing line most likely caused this Caribbean reef shark's injury below its gills.

Rarely larger than 8 ft. and 150 lbs., Caribbean reef sharks are among the most common sharks found on tropical Atlantic and Caribbean reefs.

Identified by small gills, heavy bodies and dark markings on the underside of their fin tips, these reef rascals love to steal fishermen's catches and rabble-rouse in large gangs.

They are not considered dangerous but can be very aggressive at times.

As fierce as they are, the great white, tiger and hammerhead can be shy at times. On the other hand, Caribbean reef sharks are not bashful at all, especially when there is food in the water. Once they pick up the scent, it's a mad dash to find it.

But...

after eating a little bit, they settle
down and behave, making lazy circles
around the feeding area.

This "shark parade" is a magical moment
for the underwater photographer.

A safety diver is a must when working with potentially dangerous sharks. Here, he pushes an inquisitive tiger shark away from the photograph

YOU PHOTOGRAPH SHARKS?

For starters, very carefully.

Photographers use bait to lure sharks. Without it, these secretive hunters would keep their distance.

With bait, sharks lose their natural fear of people. They compete with each other for the food and, worse, may even turn on you, thinking you're one of them!

It's important to remain alert, as cages are used only with great whites.

All sharks are unpredictable, wild animals and deserve a lot of respect.

A videographer films black-tip sharks in the Bahamas.

Accidents and Attacks

No doubt, some sharks in certain situations can be deadly. But the truth is that when they do bite, most of the time it's by mistake, as people are not part of the menu.

Tiger sharks

These rare accidents happen when humans unknowingly behave like the sharks' natural prey. At times, surfing, splashing or swimming may trigger a bite.

Even more unusual is an attack. This typically happens when a person enters the home range of a territorial shark, provokes the animal, or gets between it and its food.

Sharks usually let you know they are grumpy by lowering their fins, swimming back and forth in the same place and making tight circles. By acting this way, they are warning you:

Back off!

Food For Thought

"SHARK!" Few words in our language can cause such a big reaction, whether it's fear, fascination or both at the same time.

Shrouded in myth and mystery since humans first entered the oceans, these great fish aren't mean, killing machines, but efficient housekeepers maintaining their habitat clean and balanced. Think about it, the fur seals need the great whites as much as the sharks need them. And the same goes for all the other animals in the sea. Checks and balances; that's what it is all about in nature.

It's okay to have a few butterflies in the stomach when the word "shark" is spoken. But think about this:

1. Bees, mosquitoes and dogs are far more dangerous to people than sharks.

2. The car ride to the beach is the riskiest part of the day.

3. Your chances of getting hit by lightning are greater than getting bitten by a shark.

4. People kill 100 million sharks every year for their fins, leather, cartilage, teeth and meat.

HMMM...think about it, WHO SHOULD be afraid OF WHOM?

Caribbean reef shark

If you liked *Let's Explore Sharks*, you will certainly enjoy these titles by Batfish Books:

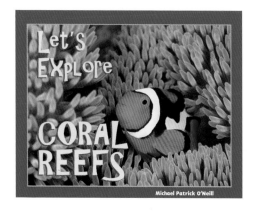

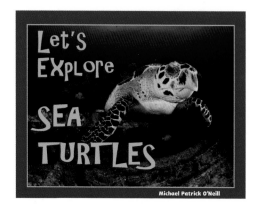

Let's go where the fish go!

Fishy Friends is sure to engage young readers. It's an intriguing and humorous account of life in the sea, as told by Charlie the Crab, the endearing narrator, and his group of wonderfully wacky and weird pals.

Fishy Friends not only entertains but also communicates the need to preserve our threatened marine environment.

In countless schools, libraries and leading conservation organizations, *Fishy Friends* is praised by educators and media specialists for its stunning photography, visual appeal, easy-to-read format and content.

ISBN 0-9728653-0-6
Ages 4-11

Home to a staggering variety of marine life, from the charismatic clownfish to the terrifying tiger shark, coral reefs are the largest living structures on Earth. Visible even from space, these rich and diverse ecosystems possess unparalleled beauty and secrets that we are just starting to unravel.

Back in action in *Let's Explore Coral Reefs*, Charlie visits these cities under the sea and explains their importance to humanity.

His words and message, coupled with dramatic images, will whet the appetite of youngsters and stimulate them to continue learning and caring about the oceans and Earth they will inherit as adults.

ISBN 0-9728653-3-0
Ages 4-11

The oceans' ultimate survivors, sea turtles have changed little since the time of dinosaurs. From the pelagic leatherback to the reef-dwelling hawksbill, these ancient mariners are perfectly designed to survive in the high seas.

Let's Explore Sea Turtles shows young adventurers how remarkable these clever creatures are and highlights the most popular species. Children learn about conservation efforts in place, and how they can make a difference protecting these adorable reptiles.

Brilliantly photographed, the book is sprinkled with revealing and useful information and will inspire kids to safeguard our precious oceans.

ISBN 0-9728653-2-2
Ages 4-11

To purchase any of these books, please visit your favorite bookstore or order online at batfishbooks.com, amazon.com or bn.com.